# SPOTLIGHT ON AMERICAN HISTORY

# Benjamin Franklin
# Writer, Inventor, and Diplomat

Michael Hesleden

NEW YORK

Published in 2016 by The Rosen Publishing Group, Inc.
29 East 21st Street, New York, NY 10010

Copyright © 2016 by The Rosen Publishing Group, Inc.

All rights reserved. No part of this book may be reproduced in any form without permission in writing from the publisher, except by a reviewer.

Photo Credits: Cover Photo Researchers/Science Source/Getty Images; p. 4 Kean Collection/Archive Photos/Getty Images; pp. 5, 20 Universal Images Group/Getty Images; p. 7 Private Collection/Peter Newark American Pictures/Bridgeman Images; p. 8 © North Wind Picture Archives; pp. 9, 10, 11, 16, 17, 21 Library of Congress Prints and Photographs Division; p. 12 Hulton Archive/Getty Images; p. 13 MPI/Archive Photos/Getty Images; p. 14 Joseph Barnell/SuperStock; p. 15 Science & Society Picture Library/Getty Images; p. 19 Bibliotheque Nationale, Paris, France/Bridgeman Images

Library of Congress Cataloging-in-Publication Data

Hesleden, Michael.
 Benjamin Franklin : writer, inventor, and diplomat / Michael Hesleden. -- First edition.
    pages cm. -- (Spotlight on American history)
 Includes bibliographical references and index.
 ISBN 978-1-4994-1784-5 (library bound) -- ISBN 978-1-4994-1782-1 (pbk.) -- ISBN 978-1-4994-1781-4 (6-pack)
 1. Franklin, Benjamin, 1706-1790--Juvenile literature. 2. Statesmen--United States--Biography--Juvenile literature. 3. Scientists--United States--Biography--Juvenile literature. 4. Inventors--United States--Biography--Juvenile literature. 5. Printers--United States--Biography--Juvenile literature. I. Title.
 E302.6.F8H47 2015
 973.3092--dc23
 [B]
                    2015018929

Manufactured in the United States of America

CPSIA Compliance Information: Batch #WS15PK: For Further Information contact Rosen Publishing, New York, New York at 1-800-237-9932

# CONTENTS

BEN'S EARLY LIFE . . . . . . . . . . . . . . . . . . . . . . . . . . . 4

BECOMING A PRINTER AND A WRITER. . . . . . . . . 6

OWNING A BUSINESS IN PHILADELPHIA . . . . . . . 8

CREATING *POOR RICHARD'S ALMANAC*. . . . . . . 10

SCIENTIFIC STUDIES . . . . . . . . . . . . . . . . . . . . . . . 12

MANY USEFUL INVENTIONS . . . . . . . . . . . . . . . . 14

HELPING HIS COMMUNITY . . . . . . . . . . . . . . . . . 16

DIPLOMAT FOR THE COLONIES . . . . . . . . . . . . . . 18

THE DECLARATION OF INDEPENDENCE. . . . . . . .20

A DIPLOMAT IN FRANCE . . . . . . . . . . . . . . . . . . .22

GLOSSARY. . . . . . . . . . . . . . . . . . . . . . . . . . . . . . .23

INDEX. . . . . . . . . . . . . . . . . . . . . . . . . . . . . . . . . . .24

PRIMARY SOURCE LIST . . . . . . . . . . . . . . . . . . . .24

WEBSITES . . . . . . . . . . . . . . . . . . . . . . . . . . . . . . .24

# BEN'S EARLY LIFE

Benjamin Franklin was born in Boston, Massachusetts, on January 17, 1706. At that time, Massachusetts was a British **colony**. Ben's father, Josiah Franklin, had 17 children. Ben was the tenth son of his father's second wife.

Ben grew up working in his father's candle and soap shop. When he was 10 years old, he finished school. He continued his education on his own by reading everything he could.

*This engraving shows the house on Milk Street in Boston where Benjamin Franklin was born on January 17, 1706.*

*This illustration shows what Benjamin Franklin looked like as a teenage apprentice when he was learning the printing trade.*

When he was 12, Ben's father wanted him to apprentice to his older brother James. James had a printing business. When Ben was 15, James created a new newspaper, the *New-England Courant*. This was one of the first privately owned newspapers in the colonies. It was a success. It helped support James's printing business.

# BECOMING A PRINTER AND A WRITER

At first Ben liked working at James's printing business. Ben loved to read the newspapers and books that his brother printed. He also spent much of his free time writing short stories.

When Ben was 16, he wanted to write for James's newspaper. His brother, however, thought that Ben was too young to be a **journalist**. Ben decided to write letters to the newspaper. He signed the letters "Mrs. Silence Dogood." James did not know Mrs. Silence Dogood was his younger brother. James liked the letters very much. He thought they were smart and funny. He printed them. When he learned that Ben had written the letters, he could not believe that a teenage boy could write so well. He was also angry that Ben had lied to him. Soon they began to have arguments. Ben decided to stop working for his brother and go to Philadelphia to start a new life.

This painting helps us imagine the day young Benjamin Franklin arrived in Philadelphia. He came without money and a loaf of bread under his arm.

# OWNING A BUSINESS IN PHILADELPHIA

Ben was 17 when he arrived in Philadelphia. He found a job as a printer. He worked very hard. The governor of Pennsylvania, Sir William Keith, wanted to go into business with Ben to start a newspaper. He sent Ben to England to buy printing equipment. When

This hand-colored woodcut shows the day Governor Keith came to see Ben Franklin in Philadelphia. He told Ben he should go to England to buy printing equipment.

This political cartoon was published by Benjamin Franklin in 1754 in his *Pennsylvania Gazette*. He published it to support his plan for the colonies to unite.

Ben arrived in England, the governor broke his promise and did not send Ben any money.

Ben worked for two years for a printer in England. He earned enough money to return to Philadelphia in 1726. In 1728, Ben and a friend bought a printing business. One year later, they began to **publish** a newspaper called the *Pennsylvania Gazette*. Ben wrote many funny stories and interesting articles for the newspaper. It soon became the most popular newspaper in the American colonies. In 1730, he married Deborah Read.

# CREATING *POOR RICHARD'S ALMANAC*

Ben Franklin liked to write books and articles under different names. In 1732, he wrote a book called *Poor Richard's Almanac*. An almanac is a type of book that has a calendar, maps, weather forecasts, proverbs, and funny sayings. Franklin published his almanac in 1733 under the name of Richard Saunders.

*These are the title pages of the 1733 and 1743 editions of* Poor Richard's Almanac. *It was one of the most popular publications in colonial America.*

*This 19th-century print, based on* Poor Richard's Almanac, *shows Franklin surrounded by many of his best-known sayings.*

People loved his book, and it was very successful. He sold more than 10,000 copies each year. This would be equal to three million copies today. He wrote a new almanac each year for the next 25 years. Even today people quote his words. One famous saying is "Fish and visitors stink in three days."

# SCIENTIFIC STUDIES

Franklin was good at many things. He was always very curious to understand how the world worked. He had a scientific mind. His many discoveries led to improvements in society.

In 1752, he performed a dangerous experiment to prove that lightning was really electricity. Franklin

This famous lithograph was created by Currier and Ives in the 19th century. It shows Benjamin Franklin and his son William using a kite and a key during a storm to prove that lightning is electricity.

*Shown here is the title page from the fifth edition of Benjamin Franklin's scientific book* Experiments and Observations on Electricity. *The book was published in London in 1774, 23 years after it was first published in America.*

made a kite with a metal wire at the top and tied a metal key to the kite string. He and his son flew the kite in a lightning storm. The wire picked up an electric **charge** from the lightning. The electric charge moved down the kite to the metal key. This proved that Franklin's ideas about electricity were correct. Franklin's writings about electricity made him famous as a scientist throughout America and Europe.

# MANY USEFUL INVENTIONS

Franklin's scientific work was always done to help human beings live better. He never patented his inventions. He wanted them to be freely available to everyone. Many of Franklin's inventions are still used today.

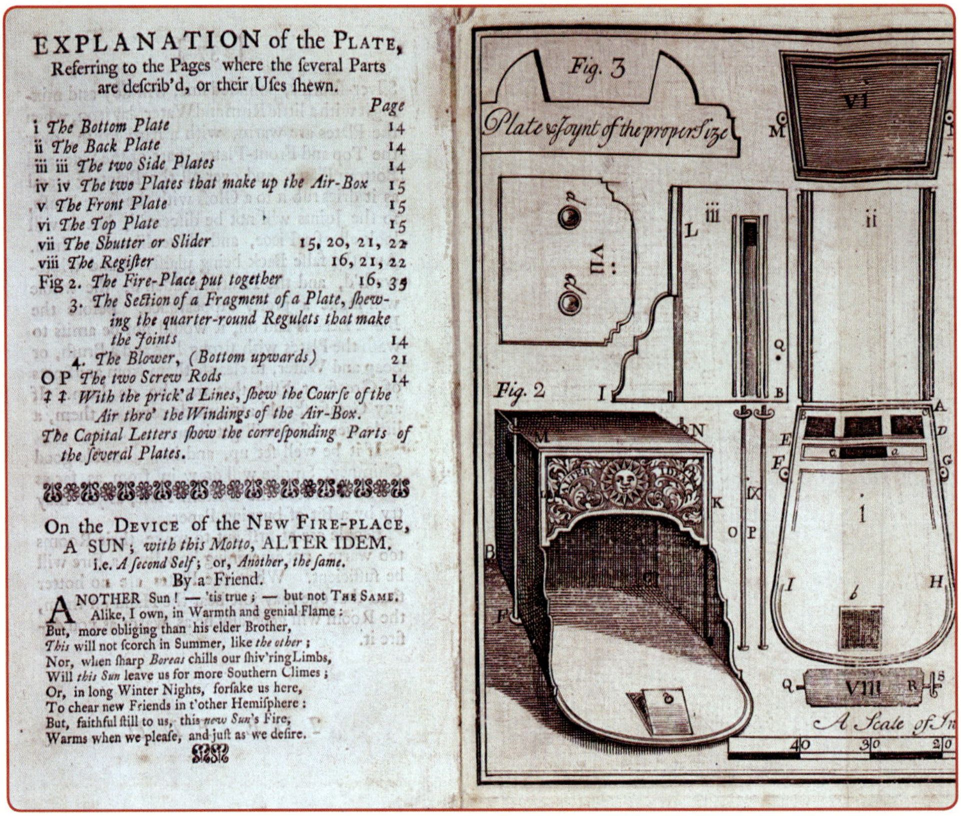
EXPLANATION of the PLATE,
Referring to the Pages where the ſeveral Parts are deſcrib'd, or their Uſes ſhewn.

| | | Page |
|---|---|---|
| i | *The Bottom Plate* | 14 |
| ii | *The Back Plate* | 14 |
| iii iii | *The two Side Plates* | 14 |
| iv iv | *The two Plates that make up the Air-Box* | 15 |
| v | *The Front Plate* | 15 |
| vi | *The Top Plate* | 15 |
| vii | *The Shutter or Slider* | 15, 20, 21, 22 |
| viii | *The Regiſter* | 16, 21, 22 |
| Fig 2. | *The Fire-Place put together* | 16, 39 |
| 3. | *The Section of a Fragment of a Plate, ſhewing the quarter-round Regulets that make the Joints* | 14 |
| 4. | *The Blower, (Bottom upwards)* | 21 |
| O P | *The two Screw Rods* | 14 |
| ‡ ‡ | *With the prick'd Lines, ſhew the Courſe of the Air thro' the Windings of the Air-Box.* | |

*The Capital Letters ſhow the correſponding Parts of the ſeveral Plates.*

On the DEVICE of the NEW FIRE-PLACE, A SUN; *with this Motto*, ALTER IDEM.
i.e. *A ſecond Self*; or, *Another, the ſame.*
By a Friend.

ANOTHER Sun! — 'tis true; — but not THE SAME.
Alike, I own, in Warmth and genial Flame:
But, more obliging than his elder Brother,
*This* will not ſcorch in Summer, like *the other*;
Nor, when ſharp *Boreas* chills our ſhiv'ring Limbs,
Will *this Sun* leave us for more Southern Climes;
Or, in long Winter Nights, forſake us here,
To chear new Friends in t'other Hemiſphere:
But, faithful ſtill to us, this *new Sun's* Fire,
Warms when we pleaſe, and juſt as we deſire.



*This detailed drawing shows how the original Franklin stove worked. The artist who drew it is unknown.*

*These bifocal glasses are very much like the ones Ben Franklin originally invented.*

    In 1744, he invented a stove made of cast iron that looked like an open fireplace. This was called the Franklin stove. It was popular because it used very little wood but gave off a lot of heat. Franklin also invented bifocal glasses. These glasses had one kind of lens on top for seeing far away and a different kind of lens on the bottom for seeing close up.

# HELPING HIS COMMUNITY

Franklin was always thinking of new ways to improve the lives of the people in his community. Books were very important to Franklin. They were also expensive. In 1731, Franklin had the idea to create a subscription library in Philadelphia. Members put their money together to buy books for everyone to read. This was the beginning of the first public library. In 1732, Franklin hired the first American librarian, Louis Timothee.

*This illustration re-creates the moment when Benjamin Franklin opened the first subscription library in Philadelphia.*

*Benjamin Franklin was the first postmaster general of the United States. This modern medal was made for the Ariel Rios Federal Building in Washington, D.C.*

Franklin created or organized many useful things for his community. He set up the first **volunteer** fire department. He also arranged to pave and light the streets of Philadelphia. He even helped to create Philadelphia's first police force.

In 1753, Franklin was put in charge of the post offices of all of the colonies. To help mail get places faster, Franklin hired more mail carriers. He had some people work during the day and others at night.

# DIPLOMAT FOR THE COLONIES

In 1757, the Pennsylvania Assembly asked Franklin to go to England to **protest** the way the Penn family governed Pennsylvania. He stayed in England for five years trying to get **Parliament** to end the political **influence** of the Penn family. He failed.

Franklin returned from Britain in 1762, but he was soon sent back. The British Parliament passed many laws to tax the colonies. The French and Indian War (1754–1763) had been very expensive for Great Britain. Parliament wanted the colonies to pay for this war. In 1766, Franklin went before Parliament to oppose the Stamp Act. He failed to get Parliament to change the law. His words of protest, however, made him the most famous champion for American interests in England. Franklin realized that the people in England did not care about what the people in the colonies thought. He understood that it was time for the colonies to be independent.

Franklin returned to America in 1775, just one month after the first shot of the American Revolution was fired. He met with leaders from the colonies to talk about the colonies' independence.

This 18th-century French engraving shows Benjamin Franklin before the British Parliament in 1766. He is opposing the taxes Parliament has placed on the colonists.

# THE DECLARATION OF INDEPENDENCE

As soon as Franklin returned from Great Britain, the Pennsylvania Assembly chose him to be its **delegate** to the Second Continental Congress. In June 1776, he became a member of the five-person committee that drafted the **Declaration** of Independence.

*This illustration was created in 1800. It shows the members of the Second Continental Congress on July 4, 1776. We see them leaving Independence Hall after adopting the Declaration of Independence.*

*This famous painting shows the moment in which Benjamin Franklin signs the Declaration of Independence.*

This document announced that the 13 colonies thought of themselves as newly independent states.

Franklin helped create a declaration that formed a new nation: the United States of America. While Thomas Jefferson was chosen to write the first draft, Franklin made certain important changes. The congress **unanimously** approved the Declaration of Independence on July 2, 1776. It was adopted by the Continental Congress on July 4, 1776, now celebrated as the date of America's birth.

# A DIPLOMAT IN FRANCE

American leaders knew that France could help them win a war against England. In December 1776, they sent Franklin to France to speak with the French king. Franklin was successful. In 1778, the French king, Louis XVI, agreed to send French soldiers to fight with the Americans. With the help of 28 ships from France's navy and the support of 10,800 French soldiers, the American army won the Battle of Yorktown in 1781. This was the last battle of the American Revolution.

In April 1782, Benjamin Franklin represented the United States in working out the terms of peace with the British. The **treaty** was signed in Paris on September 3, 1783. Franklin helped get very generous terms for the United States. He continued to work for the common good until his death on April 17, 1790. He was 84 years old.

Of all the Founding Fathers of America, Franklin is the only one to have signed the four major documents written to create the United States. These four documents are the Declaration of Independence, the Treaty of Alliance with France, the Treaty of Paris, and the United States Constitution.

# GLOSSARY

**charge (CHARJ)** An amount of electricity.

**colony (KAH-luh-nee)** An area in a new land where people live and are still ruled by the leaders and laws of their old country.

**declaration (de-kluh-RAY-shuhn)** Something that is stated or made known in an official or public way.

**delegate (DE-li-guht)** A person who is chosen to vote or act for others.

**influence (in-FLU-uhns)** A person or thing that affects someone or something in an important way.

**journalist (JUHR-nuhl-uhst)** A person who writes news stories for a newspaper or magazine.

**Parliament (PAHR-luh-muhnt)** The group of people who are responsible for making the laws in Britain.

**protest (proh-TEHST)** To show or express strong disagreement with something.

**publish (PUH-blish)** To prepare and produce a book, magazine, or newspaper.

**treaty (TREE-tee)** An official agreement, signed and agreed upon by each party.

**unanimously (yoo-NA-nih-mus-lee)** Having the agreement of all.

**volunteer (vah-luhn-TIR)** A person who does work without getting paid to do it.

# INDEX

**A**
American Revolution, 18, 22

**B**
bifocal glasses, 15

**C**
Continental Congress, 20, 21

**D**
Declaration of Independence, 20–21, 22

**E**
electricity, 12–13
England, 8–9, 18, 22

**F**
fire department, 17
France, 22
Franklin, James, 5, 6
Franklin, Josiah, 4, 5
Franklin stove, 15
French and Indian War, 18

**I**
inventions, 14–15

**J**
Jefferson, Thomas, 21

**L**
Louis XVI, 22

**P**
Parliament, 18
*Pennsylvania Gazette*, 9
Philadelphia, 6, 8, 9, 16, 17

police force, 17

*Poor Richard's Almanac*, 10–11
post office, 17
printers, 5, 6, 8, 9
public library, 16

# PRIMARY SOURCE LIST

**Page 4:** *Franklin's Birthplace* is an engraving created by J. Cole. Published by Reding & Company, State Street Boston. J. Cole was a well-known engraver and artist of the 1700s.
**Page 8:** Woodcut engraving from *The National Cyclopaedia of American Biography, Being the History of the United States as Illustrated in the Lives of the Founders, Builders, and Defenders of the Republic, and of the Men and Women Who Are Doing the Work and Moulding the Thought of the Present Time*. Published in New York 1898 by James T. White & Company.
**Page 9:** *Join or Die* is the earliest known image by a Colonist about a union of the states. It was created and published by Benjamin Franklin in *The Pennsylvania Gazette*, in May of 1754.
**Page 10:** Images of *Poor Richard's Almanack*, 1733 and 1743 published by Benjamin Franklin. He listed his own name as the person who "printed and folded" the papers at "the New Printing Office near the Market." The images are at the Library of Congress Prints and Photographs Division, Washington, D.C.
**Page 12:** *Franklin's Experiment: June 1752*, hand-colored lithograph, artist unknown. Created in 1876 by Currier and Ives of New York. Original versions of the print are at the Library of Congress, Washington, D.C.
**Page 13:** The front page to Benjamin Franklin's book, *Experiments and Observations on Electricity*, published in London by E. Cave, 1751. The book is stored at the Benjamin Franklin Collection, Rare Book and Special Collections Division, Library of Congress, Washington D.C.
**Page 16:** *Benjamin Franklin Opening First Subscription Library in Philadelphia* by Charles E. Mills. Official photographs of the painting are stored at the Library of Congress Prints and Photographs Division, Washington, D.C. The painting is owned by the Franklin Foundation.

# WEBSITES

Due to the changing nature of Internet links, PowerKids Press has developed an online list of websites related to the subject of this book. This site is updated regularly. Please use this link to access the list: www.powerkidslinks.com/soah/benf

## POINTS OF VIEW

# Should School LUNCHES Be Free?

By David Anthony

Published in 2018 by
**KidHaven Publishing, an Imprint of Greenhaven Publishing, LLC**
353 3rd Avenue
Suite 255
New York, NY 10010

Copyright © 2018 KidHaven Publishing, an Imprint of Greenhaven Publishing, LLC.

All rights reserved. No part of this book may be reproduced in any form without permission in writing from the publisher, except by a reviewer.

Designer: Seth Hughes
Editor: Katie Kawa

Cover © istockphoto.com/SolStock; p. 5 (top, background) StevePell/iStock/Thinkstock; p. 5 (top, inset) © istockphoto.com/asiseeit; p. 5 (top, girl) gmstockstudio/Shutterstock.com; p. 5 (bottom) monkeybusinessimages/iStock/Thinkstock; p. 7 Ariel Skelley/Blend Images/Getty Images; p. 9 SolStock/E+/Getty Images; p. 11 Tupungato/Shutterstock.com; p. 12 (main) fotoedu/iStock/Thinkstock; p. 12 (bread) Eising/Photodisc/Thinkstock; p. 13 courtesy of the Library of Congress; p. 15 Kathryn Scott Osler/The Denver Post via Getty Images; p. 17 Monkey Business Images/Shutterstock.com; pp. 19, 21 (inset, middle-left) wavebreakmedia/Shutterstock.com; p. 21 (notepad) ESB Professional/Shutterstock.com; p. 21 (markers) Kucher Serhii/Shutterstock.com; p. 21 (photo frame) FARBAI/iStock/Thinkstock; p. 21 (inset, left) XiXinXing/iStock/Thinkstock; p. 21 (inset, middle-right) Africa Studio/Shutterstock.com; p. 21 (inset, right) XiXinXing/Getty Images.

**Cataloging-in-Publication Data**

Names: Anthony, David.
Title: Should school lunches be free? / David Anthony.
Description: New York : KidHaven Publishing, 2018. | Series: Points of view | Includes index.
Identifiers: ISBN 9781534523326 (pbk.) | 9781534523340 (library bound) | ISBN 9781534523333 (6 pack) | ISBN 9781534523357 (ebook)
Subjects: LCSH: School children–Food–Juvenile literature. | School lunchrooms, cafeterias, etc.–Juvenile literature. | Children–Nutrition–Juvenile literature.
Classification: LCC LB3475.A6465 2018 | DDC 371.7'16–dc23

Printed in the United States of America

CPSIA compliance information: Batch #BS17KL: For further information contact Greenhaven Publishing LLC, New York, New York at 1-844-317-7404.

Please visit our website, www.greenhavenpublishing.com. For a free color catalog of all our high-quality books, call toll free 1-844-317-7404 or fax 1-844-317-7405.

# CONTENTS

| | |
|---|---|
| Free Food | 4 |
| A Lunchtime History Lesson | 6 |
| Fighting Food Insecurity | 8 |
| "No Such Thing as a Free Lunch" | 10 |
| Making Healthy Choices | 12 |
| Wasting a Healthy Lunch | 14 |
| No Longer Singled Out | 16 |
| Problems with Universal Free Lunch | 18 |
| What Do You Think? | 20 |
| Glossary | 22 |
| For More Information | 23 |
| Index | 24 |

# Free
# FOOD

Lunchtime is a fun part of the day for many students. It's also an important time. When students eat a healthy lunch, they get the **nutrients** they need to grow and stay fit. For some students, lunchtime is the only time during the day when they eat a healthy meal. They get their lunch for free because their families have a hard time paying for food.

Is it a good idea for schools to offer free lunches? Some people think it is, but others don't agree. These people have different opinions. It's good to understand different opinions before forming your own.

### Know the Facts!

The United States Department of Agriculture (USDA) is the part of the federal, or national, government that controls free lunch **programs**.

Should school lunches be free for everyone, some students, or no one at all? It's helpful to know all the facts before deciding what you believe.

# A Lunchtime HISTORY LESSON

Some students bring a lunch from home to school. Many others, though, get a lunch that's made for them at school. These lunches cost money, which is often paid by students or the adults who care for them.

In some cases, the money needed to pay for the lunches comes from the government. In 1946, the National School Lunch Act created the National School Lunch Program (NSLP). This program provides free or low-cost lunches to students whose families don't make enough money to afford a school lunch. Taxes help pay to keep the NSLP running.

### Know the Facts!

In 1966, the School Breakfast Program—also known as the SBP—started as a way to provide breakfasts to children who didn't have healthy food to eat at home.

Some people think free lunch programs should be **expanded** beyond the current NSLP to include all students. There are many reasons people support and oppose this idea.

# Fighting Food
# INSECURITY

Children need to eat enough healthy food as they grow, but sometimes that's not easy. In 2015, 13.1 million children in the United States were considered food insecure, or without enough **nutritious** food on a regular basis. Millions more children come from homes that aren't food insecure but still struggle to provide them with three healthy meals every day.

Free school lunches help these children get at least one healthy meal every weekday. For some students, a free lunch could be the only food they eat all day.

### Know the Facts!

The NSLP also helps schools provide free, healthy snacks to children and young adults in afterschool programs.

More than 30 million students **qualify** for the NSLP.

# "No Such Thing as a FREE LUNCH"

The NSLP provides free lunches to students who need them, but some people believe in the old saying, "There's no such thing as a free lunch." Although the lunches may be free for students in need, someone has to pay for them.

The government provides the money for free lunches, but it gets the money from taxpayers. Some people believe it's not fair to ask people to help pay for someone else's lunch. Others worry that the United States is in too much **debt** already and shouldn't pay more money for things such as free lunches.

### Know the Facts!

It cost $12.6 billion to run the NSLP in 2014.

Some members of the federal government believe the NSLP wastes government money. They think it needs to be fixed so people who don't really need free lunches can't get them.

# Making Healthy CHOICES

Those who support the NSLP state that it provides students with more than just free food; it provides them with free, healthy food. In 2010, the Healthy, Hunger-Free Kids Act was put in place. This act set nutrition standards for free meals in schools.

These standards were **designed** to help fight childhood **obesity** by giving children healthier food options. Students who eat healthy lunches have more **energy** and do better in school than students who are hungry or eat unhealthy meals.

### Know the Facts!

The NSLP's nutrition standards call for more fruits, vegetables, and whole-grain foods, as well as only low-fat or fat-free milk.

Former First Lady Michelle Obama played a big part in making sure school lunches met nutrition standards to help all children stay healthy.

# Wasting a Healthy LUNCH

Although the nutrition standards set by the Healthy, Hunger-Free Kids Act have many supporters, others don't approve of them. They believe the government shouldn't control what kinds of food children eat.

People who argue against free lunches for students also note that healthy food isn't always the food children want to eat. Studies have shown that students end up throwing out large amounts of the fruits and vegetables they're supposed to take with their free lunches. This wastes food instead of helping students form healthy eating habits.

### Know the Facts!

A 2015 study stated that students were throwing away 56 percent more fruits and vegetables than they were before the Healthy, Hunger-Free Kids Act.

Some people don't see the point in having free lunches if students are going to waste the food they're given.

# No Longer SINGLED OUT

Some people believe school lunches should be free for all students—not just those whose families can't afford it. Students who get free lunches sometimes feel singled out for having less money than other students. This leads some who need free lunches to refuse to **participate** in free lunch programs. They don't want anyone to know they need help paying for meals.

Making school lunches free for all students would make sure no child feels different because of what they can or can't afford. It would help students see each other as equals.

### Know the Facts!

Detroit and Boston are two U.S. cities that offer free lunches to all students in their public schools.

Free lunch for all students is also known as universal free lunch.

17

# Problems with Universal FREE LUNCH

A service called the Community Eligibility Provision (CEP) allows schools in **low-income** areas to provide free lunch and breakfast to all students. If a certain amount of students in an area qualify for free lunch, then all students get free lunch.

Many people have argued against this service. They believe that if there are some students in these areas whose families can afford lunch, those students shouldn't get lunch for free. People who oppose CEP believe the government and taxpayers shouldn't have to pay for lunches for kids whose families can afford it.

### Know the Facts!

CEP was part of the Healthy, Hunger-Free Kids Act of 2010.

Should students get free lunches if their family can afford to pay for their meals?

# What Do YOU THINK?

It's important for students to eat healthy meals. It helps them do well in school and grow into healthy adults. Some students wouldn't get a healthy meal without their schools' free lunch programs, but not everyone thinks these programs are worth the money they cost.

People have made strong cases for and against free lunch programs. After learning the facts, what do you think? Should school lunches be free? If you think free lunches are a good thing, should they be free for everyone?

### Know the Facts!

The Summer Food Service Program provides free meals to students when schools are closed for the summer.

# Should school LUNCHES be FREE?

## YES

- A free lunch might be the only food a child eats in a day.
- Free lunches help fight food insecurity.
- Free lunches provide nutritious meals that help students perform better in school.
- Universal free lunch programs help students who feel singled out for needing free lunches.

## NO

- The U.S. government's debt is too high to be paying for lunches.
- Taxpayers shouldn't have to pay for other people's lunches.
- Free lunch programs lead to wasted food.
- Universal free lunch programs waste money because not every student who's part of the program needs a free lunch.

When forming your opinion about the need for free lunches, it's helpful to consider both sides.

# GLOSSARY

**debt:** The state of owing money.

**design:** To create the plan for something.

**energy:** The power to work or to act.

**expand:** To become bigger.

**low-income:** Not having a lot of money earned through work.

**nutrient:** Something taken in by a living thing that helps it grow and stay healthy.

**nutritious:** Having things that people or animals need to be healthy and grow properly.

**obesity:** The condition of being very overweight.

**participate:** To take part in something.

**program:** A plan or system under which action may be taken toward a goal.

**qualify:** To meet a required standard.

# For More INFORMATION

## WEBSITES

**National School Lunch Program (NSLP)**
*www.fns.usda.gov/nslp/national-school-lunch-program-nslp*
This website features information about the NSLP, including its history and nutrition standards, that comes straight from the USDA.

**School Lunches: KidsHealth**
*kidshealth.org/en/kids/school-lunches.html#*
Visitors to this website find tips for making healthy lunch choices whether you buy a lunch, bring a lunch, or get a free lunch.

## BOOKS

Allman, Toney. *Food in Schools*. Chicago, IL: Norwood House Press, 2014.

Bloom, Paul. *Rules at Lunch*. New York, NY: Gareth Stevens Publishing, 2016.

Reinke, Beth Bence. *Nutrition Basics*. Minneapolis, MN: Core Library, 2015.

**Publisher's note to educators and parents:** Our editors have carefully reviewed these websites to ensure that they are suitable for students. Many websites change frequently, however, and we cannot guarantee that a site's future contents will continue to meet our high standards of quality and educational value. Be advised that students should be closely supervised whenever they access the Internet.

# INDEX

**C**
Community Eligibility Provision (CEP), 18

**D**
debt, 10, 21

**E**
energy, 12

**F**
food insecurity, 8, 21
fruits, 12, 14

**G**
government, 4, 6, 10, 11, 14, 18, 21

**H**
Healthy, Hunger-Free Kids Act, 12, 14, 18

**M**
milk, 12

**N**
National School Lunch Act, 6
National School Lunch Program (NSLP), 6, 7, 8, 9, 10, 11, 12
nutrition, 8, 12, 13, 14, 21

**O**
obesity, 12

**S**
School Breakfast Program (SBP), 6
Summer Food Service Program, 20

**T**
taxes, 6, 10, 18, 21

**U**
United States Department of Agriculture (USDA), 4
universal free lunch, 17, 18, 21

**V**
vegetables, 12, 14

**W**
wasting food, 14, 15, 21
whole-grain foods, 12